Penny Stock Trading

Penny Stock Trading For Beginners

By: Priyank Gala

Published By:

Priyank Gala

©Copyright 2015 –: Priyank Gala

ISBN-13: 978-1517565756
ISBN-10: 1517565758

Table of Contents

Chapter 1: What are Penny Stocks?

Things being what they are, exactly what are penny stocks and why are they called so? Penny stocks are not what a major speculator will be keen on. Nobody who has a lot of capital and needs to put resources into a stock is going to trouble with penny stocks.

In the event that you take a gander at the significant Stock Exchanges, you will discover hundreds or a large number of stocks recorded. These are supplies of legitimate organizations. These stocks are frequently valued by piece of the overall industry and business capital.

The majority of the shares on the stock Exchange are medium- to extensive top stocks. Their costs change however more likely than not; the costs stay inside of a certain limited band. Seldom do you see an organization do as such gravely that it gets delisted. This is the point at which it could be recorded on the pink sheets and turn into a penny stock.

Take the case of BlackBerry. This Canadian organization (once Investigate In Motion or RIM) has experienced a complete change. Only a couple of years back, it was at the exceptionally top of its alliance, and now it has wind up in a real predicament. By last check, the shares of Edge were esteemed at about $4, and it could go down considerably advance.

As per new regulations, RIM ought to now be considered as a penny stock organization. Would you put resources into RIM? Would you be willing to take a risk and contribute say $10,000 and purchase say, 2500 shares of the organization? This is the place financial specialist astuteness comes into the photo.

Who knows a couple of years not far off, the shares of RIM could move back to more than a hundred dollars, and that would make you an exceptionally rich person. Would you be willing to take that risk?

This is the thing that makes penny stocks so captivating!
You can purchase these shares for a penny and consequently the name for these shares. You will discover these shares set for about $0.30 to $0.50 regularly.

These shares are executed for not as much as a couple of dollars. This is the single greatest draw for most little speculators. There is the draw for brisk benefits also.

At the point when a little financial specialist contemplates putting resources into stocks, the first thing that rings a bell is a capital needed to buy a critical number of shares. Benefits would be irrelevant without purchasing or offering a noteworthy volume of shares. This is the place penny stocks take the middle of everyone's attention.

Would you be able to envision the amount it would take to purchase around a thousand shares of Apple Inc. Then again Google! Apple Inc. shares are going at about $500 per shares, and Google shares are at $1180 per offer. Would you have the capacity to bear the cost of that sort of cash?

You should likewise recollect that there are a large number of individuals willing to purchase and offer penny stocks. In the event that you take all these eager speculators into thought, the numbers rapidly start to make noteworthy perusing.

There is an unwarranted conviction that penny stocks are truly useless. Nothing could facilitates from reality. There are numerous illustrations of penny stocks that have had their reasonable worth expand a few hundred times throughout a couple of years.

You must recall that these are little top or smaller scale top organizations. This is the reason they are called penny stocks. Their business sector promotion is only a couple of million dollars. This additionally makes them defenseless against financial downturns like the one accomplished in 2007- 2008.

Penny stocks are additionally minimal known, as there is next to no data accessible about them. Market regulations don't oblige them to uncover data. Consequently there is next to no that speculators think about the organizations. Since the shares of these organizations are not very much managed, they are interested in expanded control. Truth be told, various bodies of evidence have been documented against representatives and merchants for fake exchanging.

This makes exchanging penny stocks a fairly touchy undertaking. As of late, there has been a great deal of buildup about exchanging penny stocks. You see a wide range of adverts on TV and radio about becoming showbiz royalty with penny stocks. You may have even gotten messages about exchanging penny stocks.

This is enticing, and numerous speculators accept what they see and find out about penny stocks. Sadly, not every last bit of it is valid. One must be cautious and channel reality from the misleading statements precisely.

Before you leave on the dangerous endeavor of turning into a penny stock dealer, it is crucial you realize whatever you can about the artistic work of purchasing and offering penny stocks. This could mean the contrast in the middle of achievement and disappointment. It could likewise mean the distinction in the middle of liquidation and dissolvability.

You must recall that there is cash to be made in exchanging penny stocks. There are various cases of individuals who have adhered to penny stocks and have wound up making a fortune.

The key thing to recollect is that there are colossal potential outcomes. The open door exists. It is dependent upon you to snatch it with both hands and capitalize on this unbelievable open door.

For the individuals who need all the more out of life, this is an open door that you just can't bear to sidestep. Such open doors don't come back over and over.

In any case, it is simpler said than done. Penny stocks are worth pennies yet before you contribute, you must recall that all exchanging is an unsafe business. On the off chance that you are arranged to go out on a limb, life is ready and waiting. Nothing generous and beneficial can be picked up without going for broke. The decision is yours.

It is dependent upon you to settle on all around educated and instructed decisions regarding the matter of penny stocks. This is the reason you have to peruse on. This is one approach to guarantee that you never lose cash with penny stocks.

Chapter 2: Find out About the Legalities of Penny Stocks

The initial phase in accomplishing riches through penny stocks is comprehension its legalities. There are such a large number of individuals who urge other individuals to put resources into penny stocks. Be that as it may, there are likewise other individuals who alert different people about being misled when they put resources into them. Luckily, the Securities and Exchange Commission of the United States of America clarified penny stocks are putting resources into its site so that everybody will be mindful and be watchful with contributing their well-deserved cash in them.

As a rule, a penny stock is a stock which exchanges underneath $5. This is the way the Securities and Exchange Commission characterizes it. Notwithstanding, a ton of speculators characterize penny stock as a stock that is exchanging underneath Si. There are additionally people who characterize a penny stock as a stock which is recorded on a pink sheet or exchanged over the counter. Moody's and Standard and Poor's distribute manuals containing budgetary reports of organizations exchanged different stock Exchanges so that speculators and brokers have a thought of how the stock will perform.

A speculator, who needs to be effective, must outfit himself with the right data. Then again, he may have a troublesome time discovering precise data about penny stocks. Otherwise called microcap stocks, organizations with penny stocks aren't needed by the Securities and Exchange Commission to submit overhauled money related articulations. Accordingly, a financial specialist may think that it hard to discover budgetary data about the penny stock organization. Besides, deceitful people may exploit the circumstance by offering questionable data around a certain organization. By hoodwinking clueless financial specialists, they gain a considerable measure of cash to the detriment of other individuals. Likewise, these penny stock organizations are known not so much fluid but rather more unstable.

Exchanging Business for Penny Stocks

Not at all like the consistent stocks, penny stocks aren't exchanged on the traditional stock Exchanges. These stocks are exchanged over the counter. They are cited on OTC Connection or OTC Release Board. The last is an interdealer citation framework which electronically shows volume data, last deal costs, and quotes for equity securities not recorded on the Stock Exchange.

A penny stock organization must be supported by a business sector producer on the off chance that it needs to be cited on the over-the-counter announcement board. It should likewise document current monetary articulations with the Securities and Exchange Commission, protection controller or managing an account controller. Albeit worked by FINRA (Financial Industry Regulatory Authority), OTCBB isn't in the NASDAQ. A ton of financial specialists are made to accept by tricksters that a penny organization is recorded on NASDAQ so they will contribute their cash on it.

OTC Connection, then again, is a between merchant system like OTCBB. It additionally offers

Correspondence abilities to its endorsers so they can arrange exchanges. Besides, it is additionally a piece of FINRA and enlisted with the Securities and Exchange Commission. With OTC Connection, securities are sorted out as OTCQB, OTCQX, and OTC Pink. OTCQB is a commercial center for securities of organizations that answer to a controller or the Securities and Exchange Commission in the United States of America. OTCQX is for securities of organizations that answer to OTC Connection and/or the SEC or US controllers regardless of the possibility that these organizations isn't obliged to submit budgetary reports. Ultimately, OTC Pink is a commercial center for securities of organizations that don't report budgetary status to any administration office or association.

The Significance of Open Data

In spite of the fact that a great deal of penny stock organizations aren't obliged to submit money related reports to SEC, it doesn't imply that they don't have a true blue business. The majority of these organizations have genuine administrations and items. Regardless of the possibility that not intended to be utilized as a part of fake exchanges, an organization which needs open data is a dangerous speculation. The cost cited for its stock may be incorrect because it doesn't mirror the open doors and dangers identified with the business and organization. Moreover, this organization might just have a little volume of stocks.
All the more critically, the absence of dependable data about penny stock organizations can be utilized by corrupt elements to exploit clueless speculators.

Misrepresentation is frequently included when there is the spread of wrong and false data.

An email spam is frequently utilized by fraudsters to hoodwink new speculators. A spontaneous email can be sent to anyone to allure him to put resources into a penny stock organization by furnishing him with false data. Web misrepresentation can likewise happen through visit rooms and release sheets. Fraudsters can conceal their personalities to lure financial specialists to purchase loads of a penny stock organization. They regularly post messages that say that they have inside data about future advancements in the organization.

Some penny stock organizations pay individuals to elevate their stock to speculators through TV and radio shows, exploration reports, and speculation bulletins. When all is said in done, these promoters likewise send reflexive mailers, messages, and spontaneous faxes. Government laws require these productions to unveil the organization or individual who paid for the advancement. Chilly calling engine compartment room strategies are additionally utilized to urge financial specialists to put resources into penny stocks. In conclusion, there are likewise flawed press discharges appropriated by fraudsters to lie or overstate around a specific penny stock.

Regular Fraud Schemes

The Pump and Dump Scheme begins with posted messages around the web encouraging financial specialists to buy the promoted penny stock rapidly before the value goes up once more. A telemarketer may call a clueless financial specialist informing the last regarding the penny stock. These promoters will urge everybody to purchase the stock because there is an approaching improvement inside of the organization. They pump up the enthusiasm to the penny stock because if the value goes up they can offer their shares. In the wake of offering their shares, these fraudsters will quit promoting the penny stock. Speculators who purchased the shares will lose cash on the grounds that the cost will fall, and nobody is occupied with purchasing them.

Some fraudsters "erroneously" leave a hot tip in someone else's voice-mail which is truly planned for a "companion". On the off chance that the collector gets to be intrigued, the same plan will be propagated like the pump and dump plan. The Offshore Scam exploits the

Non- necessity of the United States of America to enroll stocks that will be sold seaward.

The deceptive penny stock organization offers the shares to fraudsters who act like outside speculators for a huge rebate. The fraudsters will then offer the penny shares to US speculators at an expanded cost. The benefits from this false plan are regularly shared by fraudsters and some unscrupulous organization authorities. Then, the stream of shares back to the USA will bring about the offer cost to decrease, consequently to influence the ventures of real financial specialists.

Experiencing Problems with a Penny Stock Investment

A speculator who experiences issues must act instantly because the law just gives complainants a constrained time to file a case in court. He must converse with this intermediary. In the event that the issue isn't determined, then he must converse with the branch director of his intermediary. He must present a protestation in keeping in touch with the organization's agreeability division. In the event that the issue stays unsolved following 30 days, then the speculator can keep in touch with the state securities controller. He can likewise send the grievance to the Securities and Exchange Commission.

Chapter 3: Find out About Real Penny Stocks Exchanging

Before putting resources into penny stocks, a financial specialist must do his examination first. He may be urged to put resources into penny stocks on the grounds that it costs less cash, and a lot of promoters guarantee huge returns. Any individual who puts resources into it without the fundamental exploration may lose a ton of cash. A financial specialist, who can't stand to put resources into huge organizations like Apple or Google, can even now win cash from putting resources into penny stocks. The speculation is tiny, and the benefit can be good if the exchange succeeds.

It is essential not to accept each web article and email advancing penny stock examples of overcoming adversity. Penny stock contributing isn't betting. Any individual who needs to succeed in penny stocks doesn't put resources into it due to a hot tip he got from the web. He will simply lose cash if this is the situation. Penny stocks stories aren't to be trusted. A decent speculator checks the execution of the organization and additionally the cost of the stock before he puts resources into it. He must guarantee that the penny stock is encountering 52-week highs and has an in number profit development. By and large, there are a larger number of dealers of penny stocks than purchasers. Verification to this is the storm of bulletins and messages that flow in the web. Bulletins offering free tips are truly paid to advance a penny stock. A great deal of these productions makes false guarantees. Speculators must look for penny stocks that make 52-week highs on account of good organization profit and not due to advancements in different bulletins.

Usually, these productions don't advise their endorsers when to offer their stock. The cost of a penny stock can go up by as much as 30% in simply an issue of days. The system is for speculators to offer rapidly. Financial specialists who get to be covetous and sit tight for a 1,000% arrival are frequently left holding an unfilled sack. They must consider that the stock may have been pumped so they must offer the stock instantly.

Moreover, news and overhauls from the organization administration should not be considered important. It is conceivable that the administration is simply attempting to raise the cost of its stock so that more financial specialists will purchase offers. The cash can then be utilized to stay with the above water. There are situations when insiders enhance themselves to the detriment of clueless financial specialists.

Short offering a penny stock is for experts just. New penny stock financial specialists mustn't attempt it. Due to the unpredictable way of penny stocks, it is conceivable to lose no less than 50% of the capital if unpracticed speculators go short on a stock. Besides, not all penny stocks are perfect for short offering. Rather, new penny stocks speculators must set their eyes on those stocks with the high volume just. A decent benchmark is to pick a penny stock with at least 100,000 day by day volume. It is hard to offer a penny stock with a low exchanging volume. Indeed, even with penny stocks, speculators must contribute just on fluid stocks.

In numerous penny stocks, the offer ask spreads can be up to 10%, which is viewed as high. As being what is indicated, hard stop-misfortunes can bring about speculators to lose a considerable measure of cash. The best methodology is to utilize mental stops. It is best to consider the danger prize proportion as opposed to concentrating on stops. A 20% misfortune is a decent benchmark for penny stocks. Moreover, a 20% increase is a decent return. Financial specialists must offer their shares when they as of now have 20% benefits. So as to make a good benefit, they must have the capacity to pick the right penny stock. Great profit or great day by day exchanging volume is a decent criteria in picking the right stock. Financial specialists must hunt down penny stocks that have 52-week highs or if nothing else 250,000 every day exchanging volume.

Another financial specialist must practice alert in the position estimating. However much as could reasonably be expected, he mustn't exchange substantial positions. The best size is around 10% of the every day volume of the penny stock. Moreover, it is less demanding to offer a little position. Ultimately, a great penny stock financial specialist realizes that he should ceaselessly be on his toes. He should dependably make his exploration and enhance his ventures.

Chapter 4: Penny Stocks that Made Individuals Millions

Penny stocks have permitted some sagacious financial specialists to profit. Some penny stocks have developed from micro-stock organizations to huge top organizations with numerous financial specialists transformed into moguls overnight. Notwithstanding, it was not as sudden as one might want to think. Sometimes, it took truly a couple of years for the shares to go past being worth just pennies.

The vast majority of the organizations said beneath experienced turbulent times before rising more grounded. The turbulent times were the periods when the costs were basically at the absolute bottom. This was a decent time to contribute. Numerous individuals did, and they were the ones who turned into moguls a couple of years not far off.

On the off chance that you have been considering putting resources into penny stocks take a gander at these organizations and their shares. Watch how their shares have developed in quality over the long run. This is absolutely what you ought to be pondering and envisioning about.

This is the manner by which individuals make millions with penny stocks. You could be in their shoes as well.

Here are a couple penny stocks that could have made you rich.

Take the illustration of **Pier 1 Imports**. This is one organization whose shares sold for pennies lounge in the late eighties and mid-nineties.

At that point slowly as the thousand years drew closer, its share costs took off, and it came to a record high of $25. Envision what might have happened on the off chance that you had purchased ten thousand shares at $0.25 and afterward sold the part at $25 per offer.

Another that made a few individuals extremely glad was Concur Technologies.

You will be really dazed by this one. In 2001, the shares of this organization were exchanging at around $0.30, and now the value per offer is an incredible $107. Yes, that privilege. You read that effectively, this in around 13 years. On the off chance that you were sufficiently understanding, you could have made millions.

Have you heard the story behind True Religion Apparel?

This attire organization was going at 67 pennies an offer in 2004. In only a couple of years, the offer costs have soared to $32 per offer.

Look what happened to General Growth Properties. This land organization used to be in a monetary wreckage and 2009, it shares were offering at 59 pennies. Presently the value per offer is a hearty $21 and rising. There is yet another sample of what can happen when you discover shares offering for a couple of pennies. Take the instance of American Axle & Manufacturing.
The shares of this organization wind up in a real predicament amid the late money related emergency. In 2009, the shares of this organization remained at 40 pennies. Today, these shares exchange at more than $20 per offer. What a bonus for the individuals who figured out how to cling to the shares of the organization.

There are multitudinous illustrations of penny stocks that have been doing extremely well.

This is the thing that penny stocks can accomplish for you. You should simply be **PATIENCE**.

Chapter 5: Understanding Risks & Effective Risk Management

History has proven time and again that stocks, when all is said in done, has generally gone up, and putting resources into the load of an in number organization will yield an increase over the long haul, there are no ensures that a stock will go up or down tomorrow, one week from now or even one year from now. Savvy merchants know this, and subsequently they make moves to lessen their danger and accordingly stack the chances to support them, notwithstanding for transient exchanges. Notwithstanding, a few methodologies brokers use with higher valued stocks are bad systems for penny stocks. For instance, the exchanging method of undercutting versus purchasing long is not a smart thought when exchanging penny stocks.

Undercutting is the act of getting stock from a representative and offering it to another broker on the desire that the cost of that stock is going to go down, accordingly bearing the chance to purchase it at a lower cost before giving it back to the intermediary. This is unsafe with penny stocks because the liquidity, and the simplicity of discovering purchasers and vendors, is much lower with penny stocks than with higher valued stocks. This absence of liquidity can make them extremely unstable, with wide spreads in the middle of highs and lows. A short vendor can be given the shaft while a stock value duplicates or triples basically overnight. The accompanying will recognize a percentage of the variables that make exchanging penny stocks dangerous, how to assess them and how to decrease hazard.

We've officially discussed one component, liquidity. At the point when a stock is especially fluid, that implies that there is a decent supply of both purchasers and merchants in the business sector. A dealer wishing to offer shares at the business sector cost won't have some major snags discovering a purchaser. Essentially a dealer wishing to purchase shares will effectively locate a ready vendor. In the event that a stock has poor liquidity, it might be extremely hard to exchange it when you have to, as when the intra-day cost achieves an appealing low, provoking you to submit a purchase request with your representative, just to wind up having the request finished hours after the fact at a much higher than wanted cost because of poor liquidity. Another danger that is available with poor liquidity is that of stock value control. Unscrupulous merchants can buy an extensive volume of stock at a higher than business sector value, then run a fast battle of false or overstated positive press discharges to pump up enthusiasm for the stock, which then prompts speculators to purchase it at an essentially higher cost at which the beginning merchant dumps the stock on the new financial specialists. This sort of plan is called "pump and dump" and setting a base on exchanging volume can decrease the danger of succumbing to it. Another plan on the inverse of pump and dump is the short and mutilate plan. Corrupt financial specialists may short offer a specific stock, that is obtain stock that they don't claim, and pay it back to the loan specialist in the wake of purchasing it at a lower cost, subsequent to twisting the picture of the stock by starting a negative crusade of awful news, fate and agony. The volume of a stock that is as a rule effectively exchanged is a marker of its liquidity and a dealer can utilize volume to lessen hazard by just exchanging a most extreme rate of a stocks given volume at whatever time. Here are some simple approaches to decrease the danger of purchasing a stock with poor liquidity. Purchasing more than 10% of the shares exchanged on any given day is more hazardous, and purchasing a stock that reliably exchanges under 100,000 shares for every day is likewise more dangerous than not. Since the liquidity of most penny stocks has a tendency to abatement with value, a broker can further decrease chance by staying far from stocks that are not exactly $0.50 per offer, there is a lot of chance' over this cost. Notwithstanding utilizing the previously stated routines for minimizing the danger because of poor liquidity, a broker can likewise utilize the act of putting in stop utmost requests in lieu of business sector requests to purchase and offer penny stocks. A stop point of confinement request permits a speculator to place constraints on an exchange request to decrease hazard and secure benefits. A business request is essentially great until crossed out, implying that once a request is put it is filled when there is a ready purchaser or dealer, paying little respect to cost. The stop point of confinement requests gives the dealer the chance to determine a stop cost, at which time a business request is consequently put. That market request is consequently wiped out in the occasion the stock cost achieves as far as possible cost. A purchase stop point of confinement request shields a broker from purchasing stock that is over the craved cost and an offer stop utmost request shields a speculator from offering a stock underneath the fancied value, both of which are a high hazard when exchanging low volume and high unpredictability stocks. By utilizing the above systems to diminish the danger of misfortune from exchanging stocks that are of poor liquidity, brokers can improve the probability that exchanges will be beneficial.

The market promotion is one of the components that aides characterize a penny stock or a small scale top stock. This term alludes to the estimation of a recipe that duplicates the aggregate number of an organization's extraordinary shares by the present cost of that organization's stock value per offer. Financial specialists use it to assess the span of an organization as a different option for variables like income, deals or benefit. One misguided judgment that financial specialists may have is that all huge, fruitful organizations begin posting on a trade, OTCBB or Pink Sheets as penny stocks, with the relatively low market promotion. This is not genuine. Numerous organizations begin with a vast business promotion or an offer cost higher than $5 per offer. We have effectively talked about the lower furthest reaches of offer cost, yet what are the lower furthest reaches of business sector top? The SEC characterizes small scale top as those organizations with between $50 million and $300 million in business sector promotion. Organizations with not exactly $50 million are delegated nano top. While colossal additions can be acknowledged with either, a speculator can minimize hazard by exchanging penny stocks in organizations that have market benefiting from the higher end of this scale. The SEC goes down this position with the feeling that numerous smaller scale top organizations are new organizations with no demonstrated track records, new items or administrations that have yet to be completely created and business tried or have little if any advantages. In such manner, miniaturized scale top stocks are less unsafe than nano top stocks, and higher end smaller scale top stocks are less hazardous than lower end miniaturized top scale stocks. A merchant can diminish chance via inquiring about these components preceding purchasing a penny stock.

Another vital danger variable is the simplicity of which openly accessible data about the organization is accessible to speculators. As we have already examined, OTC and Pink Sheets exchanged stocks have settle for the easiest option to meet in the matter of reporting. The fundamental organizations doesn't need to make their monetary records as accessible to speculators as the organizations that are recorded on significant Exchanges do. This makes it harder for financial specialists to take after a standout amongst essential procedures of exchanging penny stocks, that of leading tireless research on the organization. While such elements as stock value, authentic stock value, exchanging volume, unpredictability, and business sector underwriting are effectively computed, different components, for example, deals and productivity are not effortlessly ascertained, or even freely accessible to financial specialists. Be that as it may, simply on the grounds that this data is not open partner accessible does not mean it can not be discovered and used to make shrewd exchanges. While those stocks that are exchanged on real Exchanges like the NYSE and the NASDAQ are moderately simple to research, and some penny stocks are, those that exchange over the counter or by Pink Sheets are definitely not. So how does one examination the penny stock organizations that are not recorded on a noteworthy Exchange? There are just three genuine techniques to direct this examination: by either creating associations with organization representatives, merchants or clients. Imperative things to ask include how representatives feel about the organization, how merchants feel about the organization's history and probability to reimburse obligations and how clients feel about the nature of the organization's items and benefits and how likely the client is to buy them once more. A cautious assessment of these variables can be utilized to lessen the danger of losing cash by buying shares of a penny stock organization. At the point when looking into an organization's suitability for exchanging, be mindful so as to glance back at the same number of bits of news as it takes to get an agreeable picture of how well the organization has done. It is additionally shrewd to take a gander at how its stock cost has responded to news about the organization. On the off chance that you can discover no data around an organization, you can diminish your danger by staying far from its stock, and then again be careful with tips, garbage messages and pamphlets that appear to push a stock or an organization, and be especially method for data that originates from huge shareholders or organization administration. A large portion of these are endeavors to pump up a stock value so corrupt speculators can take your cash. Doing your own particular exploration beats believing somebody to do it for you. Make an effort not to be enticed by the "pipe dream" examples of overcoming adversity, similar to a penny stock surging from a couple of pennies for every offer to more than a dollar in only days. This is amazingly uncommon, and a significant number of these organizations are just shells, set up so as to take speculators' cash. When you are investigating an organization, recall that next to no data around an OTCBB stock is effortlessly accessible to the general population, and no data about Pink Sheets stocks, other than noteworthy stock costs, is effectively accessible to the general population. There are special cases to this principle, especially the huge remote organizations like Nintendo and Volkswagen that we specified prior. However the greater part of those are not so much penny stocks.

Instability is an enormous danger in terms of putting resources into penny stocks. Unpredictability is additionally one of the elements that can make exchanging of penny stocks, and numerous different stocks extremely beneficial. In the realm of stock exchanging, there is intra-day unpredictability, day by day instability, week after week instability and unpredictability on a more extended timetable. A penny stock broker can leave his or her PC and return an hour later to find that a stock position saw an increment of 50% just to fall by 200% preceding the dealer had the chance to benefit from the increment. While a merchant can minimize this danger by utilizing a stopping point of confinement request, at the penance of lower increases and higher exchanging expenses, the danger can likewise be decreased by firmly observing a position. Exchanging exceedingly unstable penny stocks is best fulfilled by firmly checking the stock value so that the broker can quickly execute an exchange when the stock cost achieves a coveted offer or purchase point. Verify you have a vibe for the sort of volume that it takes for your agent's exchanging programming to execute a snappy exchange, and don't get voracious sitting tight for that to a great degree uncommon 100% increase, On the off chance that you can make a pleasant 20% to 30% in only a couple of days, you have done well and now is the right time to offer and begin once again.

Since we have inspected a portion of the greatest dangers in exchanging penny stocks, we'll proceed onward to a couple of brisk procedures for picking a decent stock.

Chapter 6: Particular Trading Strategies for Penny Stock Investing

Stock trading, particularly penny stock trading, obliges an all around investigated and created a methodology. Individuals who neglect to profit with penny stocks frequently accuse their luckiness, when as a general rule, it is not fortunes but rather a procedure, will to succeed, and order that focus achievement in penny stock contributing. All fruitful stock brokers have a procedure that they have grown before they enter the market that they strictly follow and rarely go astray from, paying little respect to normal market vacillations. The improvement of this method is a procedure, and it obliges diligent work and examination, then again, it is obviously what isolates steady victors from reliable washouts.

Understanding the significance of having a method, now you must figure out how to build up one that functions for you. Keeping in mind the end goal to amplify your accomplishment in penny stock exchanging you must have a particular system for every position you have, importance every stock you buy. You ought to know each of these methods in and out and be completely fit for disclosing to a complete beginner who knows literally nothing about money markets why you have decided to put resources into that particular stock.

While adding to your method for penny stock contributing you must take after these holy standards of contributing which are pertinent paying little respect to what sort of stock you are buying:

-Don't think all that you read around a stock, rather, look into data from numerous sources and make an educational decision based on The greater part of the data that you have accessible to you

-Never follow up on a tip unless you do your own examination on the stock first. As Jim Cramer says, "tips are for servers." Never indiscriminately take after the tip of somebody unless you completely comprehend the stock and have done your own examination!

-Figure out how to dodge bits of gossip. Again, never follow up on the talk you have caught wind of a stock. Continuously get your work done and make your own particular avocation for your position.

-Be arranged to offer rapidly. Try not to stick around and attempt to "ride it out." When your examination focuses to an up and coming decrease in the offer cost of your stock or a present decay, cut your misfortunes and escape from that position!

Once more, you ought to add to a particular methodology for each position you have. To begin with, gather and record the accompanying data for the stock.

-Exchange history

-Value history

-Late value changes/development/unpredictability

-Organization execution

-Organization Foundation

-Economic situations

Every one of these variables will help you in shaping your far-reaching exchanging system for the stock. You must study and completely comprehend the above variables precisely before shaping a technique.

Presently let's take a particular illustration.

Give us a chance to assume Sway is a penny stock dealer. Sway is frantic to profit with penny stocks. By the by, Sway should first detail a system before acquiring ANY penny stocks.

He calls his mate Jake and asks him what he has caught wind of the present penny stocks available. Jake is a badly educated speculator and goes on some of what he has heard to Sway. Sway ought to purchase 'stock X' as it is busy's most reduced, and it is required to ascend by 5% in the following five exchanging days!

Presently, Sway is a learner at this diversion and depends on Jake vigorously. He puts $10,000 in 'stock X' at $1.45 and sits tight for it to climb.

Think about what! Shock! Shock!

His picked stock falls much further. He is at a complete misfortune to clarify the occasions that prompt this monetary calamity. What's far more atrocious is that Sway does not stop and declines to haul out of the stock and cut his misfortunes, accepting that his fortunes are going to pivot in the end. Gracious yes, it does pivot, however strictly when ways stop misfortune point has been come to. Weave gets wiped out. End of story: a dismal story that could have been dodged effectively.

Anyway, what turned out badly and why? What was it that Sway neglected to do?

Sway neglected to do a principal piece of penny stock contributing, the first step! He neglected to study the value history and late value developments of 'stock X', he fizzled do his own particular homework and add to his own methodology. He followed up on a tip* from somebody and did not do his own exploration on the stock before acquiring. Had he done even a little research, he would have understood that this stock had yet far to go down before relentlessly moving move down once more. A straightforward register with the value development of the stock could have spared his neck (and his wallet obviously).

This is the first lesson you have to realize when making your particular exchanging procedure while exchanging penny stocks.

The second lesson concerns the prompt value developments. This will permit you to settle a section point. Your entrance and way out from a stock must be superbly timed. On account of the above illustration with Sway, his entrance and way out timing was truly poor. Had he entered the exchange somewhat later and in this way left when the offer cost expanded, he would have made a good looking benefit.

You must look at the latest value development and afterward enter an exchange to amplify your benefits.

ALWAYS REMEMBER THIS ADAGE.

Know The Organization!

Toward the day's end, you are exchanging shares of an Organization. Individuals regularly neglect to do research on the organization when obtaining a stock, rather concentrating entirely on the stock itself. You should likewise know all that you can about the organization whose stock you are acquiring. Without a doubt, understanding the numbers side of the diversion and having all the data on the stock is vital, yet perhaps considerably more discriminating is thinking about the genuine organization, their main goal, their objective market, their officials, their history, who is subsidizing them and so forth.

Ask yourself:

What is the business sector top of organization X ? Does it have a poor history of execution? How have the businesses reacted to organization 'X? Is there any outrage or awful budgetary news concerning the organization? Are there any arrangements in the pipeline for organization 'X'? Who is the Chief of organization 'X'? Where else has he/she worked some time recently? How did those organizations perform?

A little research will lead you to the answers that you look for. It is your ingenuity in discovering about organization "X" that will pay rich profits at last!

Had Sway tried to do his exploration, he would have discovered that organization X' had no arrangements for development and that there were minors of chapter 11.

Some of this may seem insignificant at first however recall that; it is your cash that is at stake. Should you neglect any scrap of data that can influence your money related future? You must take each bit of data you can discover, into thought when making your method for penny stock contributing in any case how imperative it may appear.

This is the means by which Sway ought to have added to his particular exchanging technique for his picked penny stock. Sway ought to have:

-Contemplated the historical backdrop of the organization 'X'. The Web is his companion regarding doing a little organization research. Practically anything you have to know with respect to cutting-RIM organizations can be found in news articles over the Web. Guarantee to peruse one, as well as a wide range of articles!

-Made a brief note of late value developments of the stock.

-Assessed the chronicled highs/lows costs of the stock.

-Attempt to focus the best passage point after cautious assessment of the value developments of the day.

-Search for any news occasions identifying with the organization "X"

-Search for any monetary information discharged by the organization lately.

This would have made Sway mindful of what was going ahead regarding the costs of 'Stock X' He would have been less reckless when starting an exchange with the above- specified 'stock X'

Had he done this, he would have presumably sat tight at the costs to move lower and afterward started an exchange with a littler sum.

In the event that you are arranged to get your work done and be quiet for your entrance point to become to, you have a genuinely decent risk of being on the productive end of a penny stock exchange.

It is difficult to add to a penny stock exchanging procedure that would be appropriate to all penny stocks and to all speculators. Every financial specialist ought to utilize the data that is accessible to them to make a system that will permit them to achieve their particular objectives for that position.

Section 7: Building up Your Strategy For Long-term Capital Gains

Exchanging stocks can be a repetitive however energizing approach to profit as an afterthought, assemble riches or bring home the bacon. As we specified in section 1, exchanging penny stocks is best left to an accomplished merchant, however, there is no precluding the charm from claiming making a speedy benefit without needing to contribute a ton of cash. The way that Penny stocks are generally shabby, and subject to large amounts of unpredictability makes them alluring to numerous dealers, particular since there are thousands, presently more than 18,000 OTC and Pink Sheets as of the date of this composition, accessible to look over.

There are truly just three essential techniques for profiting by exchanging penny stocks. These methods incorporate the long haul purchase and hold technique, the medium term exchanging system and the transient exchanging method including day exchanging. Not at all like the stocks that are recorded on the significant Exchanges, numerous penny stocks don't display great open doors for alternatives exchanging however in the event that you can locate the right intermediary and the right financial specialist you can likewise profit by exchanging choices also.

The long haul system of purchase and hold is one of the most secure and slightest unsafe systems to utilize. This procedure is best used to purchase shares of stocks in great organizations that are recorded on a noteworthy Exchange subsequent to directing watchful exploration. This technique is additionally considered quality is contributing. A stock is obtained in light of solid markers of principal money related wellbeing, a low P/E proportion contrasted with comparable organizations, a low share value contrasted with late value swings that are over the long haul moving normal however beneath the fleeting moving normal, high examiner appraisals or different signs that a stock is a decent long haul purchase. This method benefits oblige access to data that is not average of numerous OTC and Pink Sheet stocks, yet for those penny stocks that are recorded on a noteworthy Exchange this data can be anything but difficult to discover and dissect. For OTC and Pink Sheets stocks, discovering great data expected to make a long haul speculation can be more troublesome, however it is justified regardless of the extra exertion as financial specialists stand to make the most elevated picks up by picking a decent stock in another organization that stands to develop and inevitably list on a noteworthy Exchange. In the event that long haul is contributing sounds engaging, you may do a touch of additional homework and discover a penny stock that really pays a profit. This can be dubious with penny stocks because the absence of strict posting necessities permits them to figure profits in ways that can make them look more appealing than they truly are. In the event that you do discover one that looks encouraging, attempt to confirm that the profits are really paid as publicized and that different financial specialists are truly content with them. A key instrument in long haul contributing, especially for penny stocks, is the stop misfortune. Whether you utilize the programme one that your agent offers, or you set your own particular mental stop, the length of you respect it, it will decrease the danger of venture and benefits misfortune. While bigger stocks can ingest money related hardship, and in the end ricochet back, numerous penny stocks can't, making the utilization of a stop misfortune a vital apparatus for the long haul financial specialist. A forceful financial specialist with high hazard resilience may need to set a stop at a 50% misfortune in stock value while a less forceful speculator may need to utilize a more moderate 10% stop.

Medium term exchanging, here and there called swing exchanging, is a procedure used to purchase a stock at a low swing in cost with the foresight that it will go up in cost through the span of a couple of days or weeks in view of the examination of past value swings that happen on somewhat normal times of time. The danger included with this exchanging methodology is higher than that of the long haul purchase and hold method. With penny stocks, the danger is higher because of the likelihood that past value swings were the aftereffect of pump and dump endeavors, low liquidity, and low exchanging volume. These dangers make the likelihood that an expected rise in value may not come, or that it might be hard to offer the stock when the cost does go up. A dealer can secure such a speculation by using markers like moving midpoints to settle on a purchasing choice. Swing exchanging includes holding a venture position for no more than a few days, utilizing exchanging apparatuses that take the feeling of exchanging out of the mathematical statement, similar as far as possible requests and specialized examination instruments. Likewise with long haul contributing, setting stop misfortunes to execute exchanges after a foreordained drop in cost is imperative. Mechanizing the exchanging process by starting exchanges at close to a 5% misfortune or a 20% addition can minimize misfortunes and secure benefits. Your representative likely offers programmed stops by a rate change in cost or by a dollar quality change. On the off chance that you are anticipating medium term exchanging, there is truly no motivation to pay consideration on profits as you won't likely be holding the stock sufficiently long to get them. Then again, in the event that you realize that an organization is paying an authentic profit, exchanging increases can in some cases be acknowledged by obtaining the stock well in front of the profit payout, and afterward offering it when the stock cost ascends as the payout date becomes close.

Transient exchanging and day exchanging are another methodology, that includes holding a position for a brief time of time no more than a day or two, and on account of day exchanging as meager as hours or minutes. This system exploits the fleeting instability of a stock that has normal intra-day value swings and is exchanged adequate volume. Exchanging volume is critical with this method because it is so natural for a merchant to lose cash because of an absence of liquidity in a stock. Without adequate exchanging volume a merchant may enter a purchase request for a penny stock at $0.75 per share just to have that request filled after so much time has passed that the genuine price tag is much higher, say $1, the dealer having missed out on a lot of potential benefits. The same can happen with offer requests, a merchant may enter an offer request at $1 per share yet an absence of willing purchasers may keep the request from being finished so as to make a benefit before the offer value falls once more. This technique, notwithstanding keeping with the base volume of 100,000 shares for each day it , obliges that a dealer spend the whole exchanging day taking a gander at ongoing graphs on a PC screen. While exchanging instruments like stop breaking point requests can be helpful for minimizing misfortunes and securing benefits, regularly the benefits are low to the point that the included exchanging expenses of utilizing stop utmost requests exceed the benefits altogether. The included expenses can rapidly gobble up benefits of just a couple of pennies for every offer, so it is frequently better to invest the energy checking ongoing exchanging information yourself. Exchanging capital can likewise be a vital variable for day exchanging. Day exchanging is fruitful when customary, fleeting swings in the cost of a stock can be recognized and in this manner expected. These value swings are little, making it hard to make a benefit exchanging little quantities of shares. The truth of the matter is that a dealer can on any given day locate a stock that has enough unpredictability to profit by obtaining it when its intra-day cost is at a low, and offering it when it is at a high, yet it is far-fetched that exchanges will be executed at the extreme base of a low and the exceptionally top of a high. Penny stocks can vary in the middle of $0.50 and Si throughout the day, however without a doubt when an exchange is executed the real value swing may just be from a price tag of $0.75 per offer to a deal cost of $0.80 per offer. With this being a reality, even with the most tenacious brokers, day exchanging penny stocks is most gainful by utilizing all the more purchasing force, having additionally exchanging trusts available to you. This can roll out even little improvements in stock value productive, notwithstanding when a stock is inclining descending. How about we take a gander at a snappy illustration of the day exchanging a descending drifting penny stock. Say the stock opens the exchanging day at $1.20 per share, and varies at a normal $0.30 spread five times for the duration of the day in $0.05 augmentations, set from $1.20 down to $0.90, then go down to $1.15, down to $0.85, move down again to $1.10, then down to $0.70, etc.

For this situation the conspicuous method is to purchase the stock as near to the low as would be prudent and to offer it as near to the high as could be allowed, numerous times for the duration of the day. For this situation you have two variables conflicting with you, one is that the stock is slanting around So.05 per share so there is just a $0.25 spread in the middle of highs and lows. Second, the chance to benefit is restricted by the measure of time that it takes for the request to be finished. So the perfect first cycle would be to buy at $0.90 per offer and after that offer at $1.15 per offer. With $200 to spend, including say a $10 business expense, you can hypothetically purchase a little more than 200 shares. Sensibly, you won't on the grounds that it is likely that when your agent has the capacity take care of the request, the offer cost will as of now have hit the low and began to head go down. We should conservatively say that your request is filled at $0.95 per offer, so you have 200 shares after the financier expense. You watch the stock value head back upward and put in a request to offer. Your agent has the capacity offer your stock at $1. 10 for every offer, for a benefit of $0.15 per offer, $30, $30 is not terrible for a $200 speculation and a first exchange. Presently take out the financier charges at $10 every exchange and you have just a $10 benefit or 5%. In the event that you can do that 4 more times that day, averaging $10 net per exchange, you net a $50 benefit, however, will have burned through $100 on business charges. Presently you could augment your overall revenue by utilizing stop point of confinement requests, which you could have your dealer initiate at one value and cross out at another, yet to the detriment of higher expenses. A $0.90 stop would naturally enter a request at $0.90 per offer. A $0.93 breaking point would ensure a price tag of not exactly $0.93 per offer. You could utilize the same procedure on the offer request, netting generally $10 all the more in benefit, however the extra $5 per request that your agent charges for stop scut off requests countervails that $10, and there is no ensure that your request will be filled. The best wager is to exchange high volume stocks and keep a nearby watch for the duration of the day with a specific end goal to purchase and offer at foreordained mental stops to keep the feeling out of your exchanges without the cost of stop and cutoff orders. Do remember one penny stock proviso that we have not specified yet, and that will be that you ought not to utilize a larger number of stores than you can bear to lose. Additionally recall that intermittently the higher the danger, the higher the prize, and the all the more purchasing force you have, the better potential for greater additions.

Notwithstanding exchanging the genuine penny stocks themselves, financial specialists can likewise profit by exchanging penny investment opportunities. As we have beforehand examined, liquidity7 in penny stocks can at times be an issue, making it harder to discover willing purchasers and merchants without prior warning. This is much more the case with choices exchanging. Investment opportunities are an agreement that gives the agreement holder the privilege to purchase or offer a particular number of shares of stock at a particular cost before a particular date. A solitary contract is for 100 shares, the cost is known as the strike cost and the date is known as the termination date. Exchanging alternatives can be more dangerous than exchanging the hidden stocks themselves however they can likewise bring about higher increases for your cash. While a solitary offer of stock may offer for $2, a choices contract may offer for $0.25 per offer, permitting a speculator to benefit from an exchange with less cash than it would take to exchange the genuine stock. There are two essential sorts of alternatives; the call and the put. The call choice is an agreement to purchase a hidden resource at a particular cost, and a put alternative is an agreement to offer a basic resource at a particular cost. In either case, the holder of the agreement has the privilege yet not the commitment to practice the choices. Say a stock is as of now exchanging at $2 per offer, and you hypothesize that the stock will increment in cost to $3 per partake in the following a few weeks. Instead of acquiring 100 shares of stock at $2 per offer, you could buy an alternatives contract for $25 that gives you the privilege to purchase 100 shares at $200, $2 per offer. In the event that you are right and the stock does ascend to $3 per offer, you either practice your contractual right to purchase 100 shares for $200, then benefit by offering them at the business sector cost of S300, or you could offer the agreement itself to another speculator for more than the $25 you paid for it. Remember that you don't really need to purchase the basic stock keeping in mind the end goal to purchase, offer or hold the investment opportunities. The inverse is genuine on the off chance that you guess that the cost of a certain stock will fall sooner rather than later; in which case you would purchase a put choice, giving you the privilege to offer a certain stock at a particular cost. Alluding to the same anecdotal $2 stock, lets say you theorize that it will soon drop in cost to Si. You purchase a put choice that gives you the privilege to offer it at $2 per offer. At the point when the stock value falls, you can either practice your alternative by purchasing the stock at the lower value, then offering it at your choice cost, or you can offer the alternative itself the length of it has not lapsed.

The previously stated cases are approached to profit with penny investment opportunities, yet there is another approach to utilizing alternatives to secure your own penny stock exchanges, similar to a sort of protection arrangement. Since choices give you the privilege to purchase or offer at a particular cost, and on the grounds that they are such a great amount of less expensive than the stock itself, they can be utilized to fence an exchange at nearly ease. Let s consider an illustration in which case we buy 100 shares of stock ABC on the grounds that signs are that it will increment in cost from $1 per offer to $2 per share at some point in the following 3 months. We likewise in the meantime buy a call alternative for $0.25 per offer that gives us the privilege to offer our shares at the Si cost at some point inside of the following 3 months. Presently if the stock falls in value, our danger is constrained to the $25 expense of the alternative contract as opposed to the whole $100 ($1 per offer) that we paid for the stock.

While investment opportunities are not as promptly accessible for penny stocks as they are for bigger stocks, they can be discovered, exchanged and used to breaking point hazard and to benefit from either the upward or descending development of a stock without spending the cash to exchange the real stock itself. Since we have seen various procedures that can be utilized to profit by exchanging, we can proceed onward to the theme of finishing genuine exchanges, and what you will need to begin.

Section 8: Exploration on the Penny Stock Organization

When an intermediary has been picked, the speculator can converse with him about genuine penny stock contributing. He can get some information about the dangers of putting resources into a specific organization. Besides, he can research all alone by perusing the organization plan to find out about its capitalization, administration, history and how it will utilize the financial specialists' cash. When all is said in done, he can pick to put resources into an organization which will underwrite its long haul consumptions and not its typical operations.

What's more, the financial specialist can inquire as to whether the penny stock organization is presenting its budgetary reports to the Securities and Exchange Commission. He can ask for composed data about its administration, accounts, and business. He should not construct his choice in light of press discharges, talk room postings, and spontaneous email messages. Moreover, the financial specialist can ask data specifically from the organization. The speculator can likewise look for data about the penny stock organization from the Securities and Exchange Commission.

From the commission's EDGAR framework, he can know whether the organization submits reports to the SEC, He can likewise ask for such data from the Commission. A speculator is additionally urged to look for data from the state securities controller. The organization may have enrolled with the controller despite the fact that it doesn't document its reports with SEC. The financial specialist will learn if the state has approved the penny stock organization to offer its shares inside of the area.

Data can likewise be sourced from different controllers. On the off chance that the penny stock organization is a bank, it isn't obliged to submit reports to SEC. Then again, it is obliged to document its reports with a keeping money controller. Data can likewise originate from business databases and reference books. The nearby library may have reference materials about the organization. Ultimately, the financial specialist can contact the Secretary of State where the penny stock organization is consolidated. He will take in the organization is in great standing or not. Fuse papers and yearly reports can likewise be sourced from this administration office.

All together not to be defrauded, the speculator must research the penny stock organization. He must look for answers to his inquiries. He must make it a point to check with the neighborhood securities controller or the Securities and Exchange Commission. He must try to comprehend the organization's items, administrations, and business. He must redesign himself with the most recent reports about the organization. Close consideration must be paid on whether the monetary reports are examined or confirmed by a CPA. On the off chance that no overhauled data is accessible from the Securities and Exchange Commission, he can ask for it from his intermediary. He must guarantee that the data is exact and upgraded.

The state securities controller may give data about the organization's administration. Any of the administration's individuals may have run-ins with financial specialists or the controllers. The financial specialist should likewise guarantee that his merchant and his organization are enlisted and authorized to lead stock facilitating exercises. The FINRA data, likewise, it has data about business firms and other venture guide organizations.

Answers to the financial specialist's inquiries must be composed down. He must be not kidding about his venture arranges. He can observe if exchanging of the organization's shares had been suspended by the Securities and Exchange Commission because of infringement. The organization may be suspended for a greatest of 10 days if the Commission has verification that it has temperamental and erroneous data.

The speculator should likewise look at the organization's incomes against its benefits. As a rule, a penny stock organization may exaggerate its benefits in the monetary explanations. In the event that the income is low however the advantages are high, he can request clarification from the organization. The references to the money related proclamations should likewise be analyzed.

A considerable measure of deceitful plans has odd exchanges with organization insiders as Exchange of advantages for the stock or bizarre credits that may be incorporated in the references.

The speculator must observe if the evaluators don't affirm the money related articulations or on the off chance that they have noticed that the penny stock organization has the deficient cash to work the business. It ought to likewise be a warning if the organization transformed its bookkeepers suddenly. The speculator must uncover more profound to discover the reason about the change. In most deceitful plans, the organization insiders claim most of the organization offers. It is anything but difficult to control the stock cost if these insiders have a considerable enthusiasm for it. The organization or dealer may not give a legitimate answer if the speculator makes inquiries about the organization proprietorship.

At long last, if the representative can't demonstrate the data in composing, it might be a sign that the organization is into deceitful operations. On the off chance that an individual gets an icy call, he mustn't reveal his government managed savings number, his securities records or his ledgers. What's more, the financial specialist must be cautious about outside ventures particularly in the event that they are prescribed by individuals he doesn't have the foggiest idea.

Chapter 9: Exit Plan

When a request is put, the speculator must know until when he will keep the shares. He must choose to offer the shares and reinvest the cash. Ravenousness has no spot in penny stock contributing because he may encounter misfortunes in the event that he clutches his stock for a really long time.

The penny stocks business sector is exceptionally unpredictable. The stock cost can move in either heading rapidly. A fruitful penny stock financial specialist arranges his entrances as well as his ways out too because each dollar contributed is vital. However much as could reasonably be expected, the objective of the speculator is to acquire the greatest benefit, diminish misfortunes and alleviate dangers. He takes advantage in any stock value upsurge to offer his stock with a specific end goal to secure his benefits because the cost can fall whenever.

A penny stock buy must be dealt with like any high-ticket buy. A man who purchases a house needs to shop around and group data before he settles with a house he loves and can manage. It ought to be the same procedure when he purchases a penny stock. He needs to make his exploration before he makes the buy because he may wind up with a useless stock. He must have the capacity to look past the stock's polished surface to figure out any shortcomings covered up underneath.

A penny stock is regularly offered by a rising organization. Accordingly, there is very little data promptly accessible about the organization. It is exceptionally uncommon that generally coursed distributions distribute data about penny stock organizations. As a rule, the Web may not even give enough data about such organizations. In this way, it is best for a speculator to burrow profoundly. There may be sites that can offer some organization data. What he can do is to accumulate such data from different sources with a specific end goal to help him settle on a choice. He can likewise ask counsel from different sources. It is bad to get all the data from only one source. Data must be validated by different sources also. It is essential to guarantee that the speculator is getting different data from diverse sources. A penny stock organization may utilize the best showcasing official to disseminate all the colossal press discharges around the web. In the event that the same data is assembled from diverse sites, the financial specialist must suspect that its only a showcasing activity to tempt new speculators to put their cash in the penny stock organization.

Statistical surveying is vital. Data must be assembled from dependable and target sources. A speculator should likewise research the wellspring of data. On the off chance that he discovers data from a certain site, he must check the other data inside of the website on the grounds that it is conceivable that the site is simply distributed press arrivals of other stock organizations also. Then again, there are sites that offer data which its feature writer or journalist has examined broadly. These destinations can be a significant instrument for the penny stock financial specialist.

Another technique which the financial specialist may discover helpful is the point of view he gets from quotes. Essential information is regularly included in these quotes. There are sites like the OTC Markets Bunch and the OTC Notice Board that can offer important data. The speculator may get data about the stock's liquidity from these sources.

It is likewise critical for the speculator to know when to leave a position. His prosperity is not just reliant on how well he picks a penny stock, additionally on how well he offers this stock to amplify his acquiring potential or minimize his misfortunes. The way out method is most troublesome if the speculator doesn't get his work done. He may sit tight at the stock cost to go up a bit higher before he offers just to figure out that the open door may not come truth be told. A decent leave procedure empowers a financial specialist to show signs of improvement cost at the ideal time.

The price exit method searches for examples in the value development. A financial specialist generally has an objective offering value even before he buys the penny stock. When the value target is come to, he offers his shares rapidly to defend his benefits. He then puts resources into other penny stocks. The period exit method includes the timing of the buy and offer of a penny stock inside of a foreordained period. Here, the speculator chooses to offer his shares inside of a certain period with the goal that he can utilize the returns in different speculations.

The past execution exit method, then again, permits the financial specialist to offer his penny stock shares in view of the stock's recorded value pattern. The situational way out system is relevant when a news occasion or circumstance causes the financial specialist to offer his shares. He chooses to offer the penny stock after an occasion which causes the offer cost to go up. The conclusion of register methodology gives a route to the speculator to offer his shares after the day of conclusion of register for capital thankfulness, reward, and profits. The conclusion of register is the date by which shareholders get to be qualified for a reward or profit.

A way out system is a predefined arrangement or manage by which a speculator can choose to offer his open exchanging positions so he can understand his benefits. It is really more essential than a vacant position technique. This procedure can choose if the speculator wins a benefit or not. Fruitful financial specialists and specialized examiners understand its significance, and they comply with it. They are taught enough not to disregard their foreordained way out technique.

A way out technique can differ contingent upon the sort of speculator. An effective speculator settles on a way out methodology after a watchful investigation. He settles on a system which fits his monetary objective and contributing style. Consequently, he knows himself and his exchanging style even before he settles on his way out system. Any individual who doesn't subscribe to a specific way out method may think that it hard to benefit from a penny stock speculation. In the event that he has an all around characterized exchanging technique, it must incorporate a complete way out method also.

A settled way out is utilized by a financial specialist when he settles on an altered benefits rate before he offers his shares. He doesn't offer his stock unless that certain benefit rate is met. The principle drawback of this method is that the innovator doesn't offer regardless of the fact that the stock cost is persistently falling. Besides, the stock value might consistently go up after he has sold his shares when his preset rate has been ruptured.

The trailing stop exit system is really a stop request which teaches the exchanging stage to consequently offer the financial specialist's shares at a foreordained cost or rate. In the event that its a long position, the trailing stop can be set beneath the present stock exchange cost. On the off chance that it s a short position, the trailing stop is set over the present business cost. This methodology ensures the speculator's benefits by keeping up the vacant position if the value course is great.

Something else, the way out technique will be executed by the exchanging framework.

The dynamic way out system is all the more normally utilized by financial specialists who follow7 a pattern. Its objective is to secure the benefit. In this system, the financial specialist exploits an inversion sign to trigger the way out method. The decision of pointer, for the most part, relies on upon the financial specialist's exchanging methodology. Much of the time, one, and the only marker is utilized to trigger passage and way out systems. For a way out methods to be compelling, they ought to match the picked exchanging technique of the financial specialist. The financial specialist can make a back-test before he utilizes any of his picked systems in live exchanging.

As a rule, a financial specialist either clutches his stock for a really long time that he loses a great deal of cash, or he exits too soon and misses the opportunity to acquire more cash. Financial specialist apprehension and voracity must be overseen with a specific end goal to succeed in penny stock contributing. The right leave technique must be set up with a specific end goal to keep human feelings from demolishing the venture opportunity. Consistency is additionally vital so as to turn the chances in the speculator's support.

Position size is noteworthy in any penny stock venture. A great deal of financial specialists doesn't register the right exchange size at any given position. In actuality, the financial specialist can't be correct constantly. He may lose some of his positions. So as to guarantee achievement, he must have the capacity to minimize such misfortunes with the goal that he doesn't lose a considerable measure of his well deserved the cash. His position size must be reliable with his speculation objective and exchanging style. The aggregate position size must be restricted. This sum may be not quite the same as the aggregate sum of cash the financial specialist can contribute on an exchange. Case in point, the financial specialist can contribute 10% of his record adjust on an exchange with 5 positions. In the event that the record parity is $10,000, he can open 5 distinct positions at

$200 each. In this way, a misfortune in a position can be balanced by alternate positions.

Besides, the speculator must have a preset most extreme danger. This rate must be set to a most extreme of 5% for every exchange. This implies that a speculator is willing to lose at most 5% of his record offset to any specific exchange whenever. In this manner, the $200 interest in a given exchange the past illustration is still beneath the 5% most extreme danger rate of $500.

Before starting an entry position, the financial specialist must know his wanted benefit and the timing of his way out. It is judicious to look for a benefit in any event thrice its hazard. Overseeing dangers and prizes with the right position size can make an effective financial specialist.

Chapter 10: Identifying Profitable Penny Stocks — The Do's & Don'ts

One truly awesome approach to increasing some exchanging knowledge is to utilize one an online stock exchanging test system or diversion. These recreations permit you to set up a reenacted exchanging record, which is supported with reproduced cash, as a rule, $100,000. There are various sites that offer them, as Forbess investopedia.com. The Wall Street Journal's marketwatch.com and Market Watch's vse. Market-Watch. com. On the off chance that you need to sign up for one of these free records, visit the site and take after the connections to the test system and sign up page. There a couple of essential fields that will request data like name, email location, and watchword. Make sure to experience any of the instructional exercises offered, so you know how to utilize the test system. The procedure of making exchanges is extremely straightforward and like how genuine web is exchanging programming functions. The stock image of the organization's stock you need to exchange is gone into the fitting field, alongside the quantity of shares. On the off chance that you are entering a stop request or point of confinement request (a few test systems won't have this alternative, so verify you sign up for one that offers it) you additionally enter an objective cost. When the request is entered, you will have the capacity to preview7 it before it is set. Most test systems offer the essential elements of any online dealer and are anything but difficult to utilize. There are likewise research devices that give a point by point and constant quotes; you can gaze upward organizations by name or stock image to lead research and audit organization data and history, including memorable stock. One admonition is that not all test systems permit exchanging penny stocks, but rather it is basic to let dealers exchange down to $2 stocks so you will have the capacity to get some experience. On the off chance that you are accustomed to exchanging stocks as of now, a test system is still a decent approach to practice methodologies for picking and exchanging penny stocks.

We quickly touched on the subject of exploration in section 2, and how it can be an element that diminishes hazard. The act of directing nitty gritty examination into an organization before purchasing its stock is a key to picking a decent stock. One of the simplest approaches to distinguish a decent penny stock is to contemplate its noteworthy value and exchanging volume outline through the span of one year. There are various examples that you can distinguish that may be pointers that the stock is a decent pick, and one of the most effortless of these is its 54 week high. A 52 week high is the most astounding value that the stock has ascended to in the previous 52 weeks. A stock that is at or close to its 52 week high is a decent stock to pick, the length of you can wipe out the likelihood that it is at that high just because of false, deceptive or exorbitant positive press discharges and different strategies that are utilized to prop up an organization's stock cost. In the event that you can locate a stock that has reliably ascended throughout a year to a 52 week high, with for all intents and purposes no press scope, press discharges, editorial from administration or other attention, that stock may have the capacity to make you a snappy buck, especially on the off chance that it meets a percentage of the other danger diminishment variables we examined in section 2. Exchanging volume ought to meet the 100000 shares for every day least (this may be a normal over a year), and the cost of the stock ought to be no not as much as a large portion of a dollar. Be cautioned then again, that reliably discovering penny stocks that meet these criteria is troublesome, especially on the off chance that you are looking outside of the real trades; at either OTCBB or Pink Sheets. When discovered, however, this sort of stock can without much of a stretch deliver a 10% to 30% addition.

Keeping in mind the end goal to pick a decent stock, it is advantageous to have a grip on how the hard quantities of an organization can effect stock costs. Quarterly and yearly deals figures, organization profit, obligation to pay and resource for obligation proportions, and even master examiner redesigns, downsizes, and suppositions are a decent place to begin. Utilization alert when assessing such data when it originates from known shareholders, however, it can pay to know who is purchasing a specific stock and why. You may find that this data is uncommon and elusive for penny stocks, especially those that exchange on the Pink Sheets. Dissimilar to a significant part of the data that is promptly accessible on the web, this sort of data is infrequently just a couple clicks away and may take some genuinely profound burrowing to discover; thus, it is gainful to just put resources into organizations that work in an industry or business sector area that you have great learning of. There are some great assets for data on penny stocks that aren't recorded with a noteworthy trade. PTC Markets shows cites, chronicled information, organization press discharges and budgetary filings, stock diagrams and all the more on a large number of OTC stocks, including Pink Sheets. OTCBB is a comparable site. However it doesn't have data on Pink Sheets stocks. These sites are awesome for looking into and screening stocks, however so as to get to ongoing quote information you should pay for a membership.

There are various specialized investigation considers that can be utilized to pick a decent stock. These are given numerical equations and capacities that utilization variables, for example, stock value, exchanging volume, the number of days that an offer value shuts up versus down, organization profit and others. One such investigation is known as the relative strength index (RSI). This record is a number in the middle of o and 100 that is taking into account a proportion of days that a stock value closes higher to days that it closes lower. The RSI is utilized to focus when a stock is considered overbought or oversold and can be a decent pointer of when to purchase and when to offer a stock. Numerous merchants consider a purchase sign to be the point at which the RSI moves over the 30 level and an offer sign when it moves underneath a 70.

Specialized investigation of a stock is best utilized for picking a stock when numerous strategies are joined. Another examination device that can be valuable is one called a moving average. A moving average is called only that in light of the fact that it is one an average of a stock's end cost after some time and two on the grounds that the time of the normal itself moves. How about we take a gander at a basic 10 day moving normal first: the normal shutting cost of a stock is ascertained over the former 10 days, days l through 10. This average is shown as an information point on a diagram of the stock's value per offer. The following information point is the next day's 10 day normal, that of days 2 through 11, then days 3 through 12 and so on. A moving normal can be processed for various time reaches, similar to 10 days, 20 days, 50 days and 200 days. A 200 day moving average is processed for quite a long time 1 through 200, then days 2 through 201 etc. Numerous merchants utilize short term moving midpoints to recognize fleeting patterns and long term moving averages to distinguish long-term trends. These in themselves are not so much good but rather or undercut markers however when a term moving normal is utilized as a part of mix with a long term moving average they can be utilized to show a decent time to purchase or offer. At the point when the short moving average falls beneath the long term average, it could show that a descending pattern is nearing, setting off an offer sign, and when the short term moving average transcends the long term average it could demonstrate a decent time to purchase in light of an up and coming upward pattern. Similarly as with the greater part of the danger components and the stock picking routines effectively examined, the moving average is best utilized as a part of blend with different variables to lessen hazard and pick stocks. In the event that you find that the elements you are utilizing to settle on exchanging choices for a specific stock are in clash, it might be best to stay away from that stock and search for one with great markers and generally safe that exceed the awful pointers and high hazard.

Another variable that can be demonstrative of a decent stock to exchange is a stock's cost to profit (PE or P/E) proportion. The cost to profit proportion is essentially an assume that is ascertained by partitioning a stock's offer cost by the fundamental organization's income per offer (profit over a 12 month period separated by number of shares of stocks). There are two fundamental P/E proportions; the trailing and the forward. Trailing P/E is figured utilizing the past twelve months profit number and forward P/E is ascertained by including an evaluation of future income, whether that be month to month, quarterly or a year into what's to come. P/E is utilized by financial specialists to figure out if a stock is underestimated or exaggerated. A stock with a low P/E contrasted with different organizations in a specific industry or area may be thought to be underestimated, and this a decent purchase, especially if the organization is fiscally showing improvement over comparable organizations. Higher P/E proportions contrasted with comparable organizations can be a pointer that the stock is exaggerated and ought to be sold, or that different financial specialists have a high trust in the stock and it ought to be looked at a huge drop in cost some time recently purchasing it.